TO: _____

Don't be S.A.D

From: _____

Don't Be S.A.D:
A Single Parent's
Guide to Finding
Your H.A.P.P.Y

INGRID M WILLIAMS

Don't Be S.A.D: A Single Parent's Guide to Finding Your H.A.P.P.Y
Edited by Khalya Hopkins, M.A., M.S.Ed

Copyright © 2015 by Ingrid M Williams

ISBN: 0692387277
ISBN 13: 9780692387276
Library of Congress Control Number: 2015902688
Ingrid M. Williams, Orange, NJ

DEDICATION

To God – I thank you for your love, mercy, grace, and provision.

To My Amazing Daughter (ZLH) – You have saved my life in ways you will never know. Thank you for making me a better woman, mother, and friend, I Love You.

To My Parents – Thank you for providing a north star that I can always follow when life gets rough.

To Everyone Parenting While Single – Don't give up!

CONTENTS

PURPOSE OF THIS BOOK

I penned this book with one specific purpose. To help parents that have recently become single realize their potential to be great parents and people. To realize that you can have an abundant life even during this time of parenting while single. In fact, although it may not be the most ideal situation, you just may find yourself during the process.

There are many reasons why a parent may have to check the single box next to their relationship status: a bad break-up, death, divorce, the list could go on. Dealing with any of these things is hard to do when no children are involved. Add some children into the mix; things begin to seem almost impossible to endure. Often times we tend to get very S.A.D. in dealing with the transition. This sadness, if left untreated, only creates more pain and difficulty in our lives. I know because I've lived it. I am and have been parenting while single for over 9 years. I stayed S.A.D. for about the first five years then one day, I made up my mind that I had to reclaim my life and in return, help as many people as I could. In dealing with the transition of parenting while single, I realized that not only was feeling S.A.D. an emotion, it also became the acronym for the top three emotional turning points I and most of my friends that are parenting while single have gone through. They are **Shock, Anger, and Defeat**.

My approach to this topic won't be about how I did everything perfectly. It will not be to tell you how you need to let go of the past and move on (although moving forward is a necessary step). My purpose is to let you know that the feelings you may have are real and they are nothing to be ashamed about. However, these negative emotions often make your situation worse. Being S.A.D. for too long was the worst mistake I've made in my journey of parenting while single. I had to start looking for my H.A.P.P.Y. and embrace my new life, my daughter, and our dreams. I will take you on the journey to H.A.P.P.Y. as we continue through this book.

I will walk you through each step as I experienced it and what helped me move past each one. Now don't beat yourself up if you just don't snap out of whichever phase you find yourself in right after you read each chapter. Remember these are steps I've taken and lessons I've learned over the past six years. The truth is I have to fight myself daily not to allow myself to go back to some of the darker emotional places of not wanting to face the world. I've slept whole weekends away, lying to my family and friends about having plans when I was really at home in bed for days at a time. I've fought the urge to take my life several times and more than once I've found myself with the tools in hand to actually carry out my plan. Every morning I wake up, I look into the mirror and tell myself I can make it. My hope is that you will be able to identify with some part of this book and can honestly start the road to healing. There is a wonderful life out there for you way beyond the dark place you may be in now. I hope this book will help you 1) recognize where you are emotionally 2) give you a great starting place to help you move forward and 3) help you become the strong, loving parent that you were created to be.

Remember single is your relationship status, not your parenting status. You are always charged with being the best parent you can be and nothing can change that.

1

SHOCK

A sudden or violent disturbance of the mind, emotions, or sensibilities: dictionary.com

Let me start by describing who I once was: a talented, college educated young woman who had dreams of conquering corporate America, and jet setting through life. Having children was something that I saw myself doing with my perfect husband, in my perfect house, working my perfect job, and living off our perfect bank account. So you can imagine my shock when I discovered I was with child in the bathroom of my perfect apartment, while being employed at my not so bad job, while dating and living with my sometimes perfect boyfriend, with a barely okay bank account. That was the kick-off of a series of shocking events.

I will give you the abridged version of the next series of shocks because I am trying to move past the past and I don't want to cause any unnecessary hurt to other parties involved (that's what I call growth). However, here is a little background. Although I was excited to be pregnant, the timing wasn't as perfect as I wanted it to be. My live-in boyfriend and I had a plan and he had goals that involved the possibility of him living away for a while to complete them. My pregnancy presented a new factor in the plan. There was one thing I knew and that was that this child was special and deserved a chance. In my effort to be supportive, I went on with our previous plans not really wanting to rock the boat or wanting to be resented for not allowing my boyfriend's life-long dream to be manifested. I put on my brave face and tried to prepare the best way I could. My boyfriend went on to pursue his goals and I supported him. Although there was a part of me that wanted to scream STAY, he was gone and this is when the reality of my situation hit and hit hard. When he first left, I really thought we were in it together. It didn't take long to realize that I was totally in this parenting journey alone. After the first couple of weeks, I realized that out of sight equals out of mind. My daughter was 4 months old and I found myself parenting while single and dealing with full force post-partum emotions. In addition, I had to accept the hard facts that the person that I trusted the most, the man that I created life with, was gone. I just couldn't believe it. I had too much intelligence for this. I had a "good" job; I was a "good" girlfriend, and I was a "good" mother. Why was this happening to ME? I was trying to find the answers to this question and pondering the statements listed below on a daily basis. My quest to answer these questions started my journey to some deep emotional pitfalls. Do you find yourself thinking these types of thoughts?

1) I can't believe this happened to me.
2) How could he/she have done this to me?
3) I wasn't supposed to be parenting alone.

Sound familiar? Well I stayed shocked for about 6-8 months or at least that's where I stopped counting so it really could have been longer. The shock started to affect my whole life, work performance, household duties and relationship with my little one, family and friends. I was numb to all things and I couldn't function daily because in my mind I was constantly trying to search for the answers to the series of questions and thoughts that were playing through my head.

Looking back through the process I recognized that this phase was when I embarked on my career as an amateur actress. When I was out amongst people I would act like I was a strong woman and mother that had it all together and I could handle the situation that I found myself in with grace and dignity. In reality, I was in the starring role of fighting for my life and to do so I had to take on several different personas. I will speak of three: **The Great Pretender**, **The Perfect Victim**, and **The Cripple.**

It was during this shock phase that I began my performance as The Great Pretender- everything was fine, and I could handle it. I pretended that I was making every effort to carry out my duties as a mother. That I had rolled up my sleeves to fight through this rough time and I was emotionally equipped to do it. I thought at the time, *Yes, I am alone with a newborn and a dog, but I am fine, I can handle it. I don't know how I am going to buy formula and pampers but I am fine. The rent is starting to get paid later and later after the 1ˢᵗ, and sometimes in portions but I am fine.* I found myself functioning only the days that I had to work. I would spend weekends alone, in bed with my daughter, not going anywhere or speaking to anyone, barely eating, and lying about plans that

I didn't have to friends and family as to not draw concern be-cause…..you guessed it, I was FINE. What I discovered (not so quickly) was that pretending that everything was fine made life harder. It created a false reality to those that may have wanted to offer help that their help wasn't needed. I really only wanted the help of one person. The reality that I wasn't able to face was that he was unwilling to help with anything. So instead of allowing my family and friends to help where they could, I cre-ated a boulder of weight to carry on my back, and my back was quickly breaking. Pride was one of the biggest reasons for this. I felt that if I let others know how much help I really needed, I would be admitting to my own failure. After all, I had cho-sen this relationship; I had accepted this treatment, and there was even a time that I fought against my family in defense of my relationship. So the feeling of deserving exactly what I was receiving overwhelmed me. I was so ashamed and I felt so be-trayed. How could I have found myself here and left alone with a small child? I had two college degrees and a good job and didn't fit the "typical description" of what the media portrays as a struggling single parent. I couldn't bare the humiliation of communicating to others that my life wasn't working out as I had "planned" it and I didn't know what to do to get back on track. This proved to be however one of the fastest things that sent my life spiraling out of control. While I was pretend-ing that everything was okay, I had checked out of reality. The bills piled up while my self-esteem plummeted. I was drown-ing in emotions and the only words that I could muster when asked how I was doing was "I am fine". It was like an out of body experience; I felt like I was watching myself from above, screaming to myself to snap out of it and ask for help but I just couldn't. I couldn't snap out of the fog of what had become my life. The more I tried, the harder it was to face what my reality had become. I was scared; I was hurt, and I didn't know how to process all the emotions I was feeling at once. Honestly, it was easier to just check out and not deal with anything.

Signs that you may be in the shock phase:

1) Trying to hide or mask the reality of your situation to others
2) No motivation to complete the daily tasks of parenting and household maintenance
3) Not opening mail or keeping up with bills
4) Not actively participating with family and friends

Suggestions to help you get through the shocked stage:

1) Admit how you are a feeling to a family member, close friend, and/or professional.
2) Get out of the house as much as possible, even if it's just to the park with the kids. Fresh air really helps you think and process.
3) Incorporate some ME (My Exhale) time into your routine. Time to regroup will help you clear your mind. ME time can be as simple as having your lunch break alone once per week.

2

ANGER

A strong feeling of displeasure and belligerence aroused by a wrong; wrath; ire. dictionary.com

I entered this stage once the initial shock of my situation began to wear off. I finally had gotten some feeling back and what started out as feelings of hurt, betrayal, and rejection quickly turned into anger. I needed to make sure that the hurt and pain I felt was felt by my ex and I was pulling out all the stops. It's during this phase that I unleashed the most deadly venom. The anger I began to feel toward my ex, my life, and myself, and at that time my child was totally destructive. I have done things that I never knew I was capable of in an effort to try to bestow even the smallest portion of pain that I had felt onto my ex. The pain of the rejection I felt had turned into an uncontrollable inner rage. It was during this phase that I became the Perfect Victim. I would tell the story of all that had been done to me by this horrible man even after all I had given to him, to anyone that would listen. I honestly ruined a number of good dates because I was so caught up in being the victim.

I was addicted to the attention and sympathy that I received every time I shared with someone my version of the events that allowed me to end up parenting while single. What I didn't realize was that being the victim didn't allow me to grow, and the longer I stayed in the place of hurt, my hurt turned into anger toward my ex. To my surprise, that anger would also grow into subconscious anger toward my daughter and ultimately me.

Anger is addictive like a drug. There is a high that you feel once you start on a quest to seek revenge that is temporarily satisfied by small victories, but after each one, the moment of fulfillment only lasts a second and the pain and rejection sets in even more. Instead of feeling fulfilled, you just feel empty and lost. I realized that even though I may have hurt my ex with the sharp things I said, or by some other act of revenge I committed, it never left me satisfied; it just caused more problems when it came to co-parenting and moving on with my life.

As a result, I just ended up looking crazy. Although my sole purpose was to make him feel a little bit of the hurt I felt, he really just thought I had totally lost it, which caused me to be mad at myself for even getting to the point where I would have acted so out of my character. I quickly realized that my anger really wasn't toward him; my anger was with myself for all the times I should have spoken up during our relationship. Trying to keep the peace and be a "good" girlfriend had left me voiceless and living a life that I felt I no longer had control over. I was now trying to exercise my voice in an unhealthy manner that really was more harmful than helpful.

My anger toward my ex spilled over to anger at being a mom. Let me state first and foremost that I love my daughter more than anything and I would never do anything to consciously harm or hurt her. However, at the time I was so hurt and so angry that my parenting style reflected just that. The feeling of, *if it wasn't for him I wouldn't be in this mess,* began to eat away at how I viewed my role as a mother raising the child of the man that had completely abandoned me when I needed him the most. Now I was here struggling with this child all alone, while he took no responsibility for the life that he created. These were the negative thoughts that consumed me daily and continued to feed the rage that was stirring up inside me.

The built up anger caused me to lash out at her when she had little kid moments like making a spill, or moving slowly or asking numerous questions. I found myself not being able to emotionally connect at times. The anger consumed me and left no room for me to love so I'd just yell. My temper was short and I had no patience. My poor daughter was afraid of what my reaction would be when she made even the simplest mistake. Not that I would ever hurt her, but even the yelling and lack of sympathy or compassion had left her unsure of what my reaction might be at any given moment.

I got my wake up call one day when I watched my daughter become paralyzed with fear after one of my rants. She was completely unsure of herself, what to do next, and what my response of her next move would be. I went into the bathroom, broke down, and prayed to God to change my heart. I no longer wanted to be the angry mother. I wanted to love, enjoy, and have fun with my daughter. After all, we were on this journey together, just the two of us and being angry all the time was creating a hostile environment for us both. The reality was that my "journey" is actually my daughter's life and I need to provide her with a life filled with happiness, joy and love. The world is hard enough, and home should be a safe haven for our children and it's up to us parents to create it no matter what.

This phase is one that you may slip in and out of a little more frequently than you would like, especially if you are co-parenting. Co-parenting for me means working collaboratively with the other biological parent to successfully raise a productive human being from two different households. You have to consistently condition your mind and heart to not harbor anger. Anger is a deadly emotion. It causes unintended harm to yourself and others and it blocks your view of all the good things that are around you. It is in your best interest to come up with a way to transform your anger into positive energy. If you feel yourself coming into an angry place I suggest movement. If you are face to face or on the phone with the person who is making you angry I suggest you quickly end the conversation and change your environment. It's hard to clearly communicate your thoughts once anger sets in. Go for a walk or run. Turn on some calm music, or maybe take out your journal and jot down your thoughts.

To help me eliminate my anger I had to become thankful that I had the honor to be able to build a deep one on one bond with my daughter. I had to begin to think about the great privilege I had been given to be able to provide my daughter with all of my undivided attention. I was able to really focus on her needs, and get to know every aspect of who she was, uninterrupted. Yes, parenting solo is hard at times but you have the privilege and the honor to share and create lifelong memories with your children on a daily basis and that is worth so much more than being angry all the time. It's a matter of perspective. Don't continue to waste precious time being angry at the fact that you are currently parenting while single when you could be using that time to create memories with your children. Use that energy to forgive yourself, make peace with your past, and remember that the love you have for your child(ren) is pure and allow your choices to be reflective of that.

Suggestions to help you when you find yourself in the angry stage

1) **Be honest about what you are truly angry about and why.**

2) **Be honest about who you are truly angry with and why.**

3) **Write a letter to the person you identified as the root of your anger. List everything you are feeling and why. Then destroy it.**

4) **Use prayer and meditation to help replace thoughts of anger and rage with those of love and peace.**

5) **Volunteer to help those in need. Helping others is a great way to gain a new perspective.**

6) **Keep a journal - freely write down your thoughts and feelings as they arise.**

7) **Record your thoughts –when you're angry, when you're sad, when you feel like you are going to flip out, record the thoughts that you are having. Listen to the playback and ask yourself what does this person sound like? If you were watching this person on TV, what would be your reaction to**

him/her? Sometimes we get a clearer understanding of what is going on inside of us if we can hear what our thoughts sound like.

3

DEFEAT

To eliminate or deprive of something expected: diction-ary.com

This is what I'd like to call the black hole stage. It's the place where you feel as if you are being suffocated by your own life. If you are not careful, you can spend way too long in this stage. Some people lose their life here, and others never move beyond this point. You feel like you have lived your best days and you don't have the time, energy, or drive to totally recreate a new life.

I entered this stage and stayed here for a good, long while- years to be exact. I can honestly say as I sit here writing this book that I dragged myself out only more recently than I'd like to admit. It is at this point where I took on my final persona as The Cripple. I was not crippled physically, but emotionally I was paralyzed and it caused a series of in-action that made life even more difficult. The unpaid bills, the stresses of parenting and work, and the rejection that came with the break up, reduced me to the point where I had no fight left. I was physically and emotionally drained and all I could do was watch life pass. I woke up every morning going through the motions of what looked like living but on the inside I was hollow- emotionally depleted with no feeling of any self-worth. I had allowed myself to be stripped down to a shell of the person that I formally knew. I was living in the mindset that what I had to offer just wasn't good enough; that I had given my best and it was rejected. It made me feel worthless that little ole me could never provide the things that I needed for my daughter to ensure that she lived a better life than I had. I was raised by both of my parents and had a great childhood so I feared that my daughter would not have the same experience because I was raising her alone. I had bought into all the stereotypes and statistics that stated that woman-headed single-parent households are destined for poverty, and if I didn't have someone to help me that I could never do it alone.

The feeling of defeat crippled me. I created a world that totally didn't exist. It made my own load much harder to carry all because I felt like I had no arms, muscle, or back to bare it. What I had to realize was:

<u>Defeat is A LIE!</u>

You can do anything that you put your mind to and that's how I'd like to end this chapter. You are not defeated. You are not weak. You are not worthless. You are on your way to a beautiful life- it's waiting for you. If you can identify with any of these stages, I hope to start you on the journey to finding your way to H.A.P.P.Y.!

Be H.A.P.P.Y.

Now that we have identified what makes you S.A.D., let's begin our journey to H.A.P.P.Y.-**H**onesty, **A**ppreciation, **P**rayer, **P**urpose, **Y**ou. The path isn't always pretty. You will have to confront some of your greatest fears, some of your ugliest truths, and some of your deepest pain. At times it won't be easy; you'll want to give up. Don't give up! Push through it! The life that you will find is far greater than you can imagine. It will be worth the journey. You deserve to live the life that you envision. The only person that can create that life is you.

Let's start on our road to H.A.P.P.Y.!

4

HONESTY

Truthfulness, sincerity, or frankness: dictionary.com

The first thing I had to do was be honest with myself, my feelings, and my situation. I loved my family; I didn't want the relationship to end but it had to-for the betterment of me, my child, and whatever relationship was left of me and her father to raise her. It hurt like hell. It wasn't easy, and I was lonely. I wasn't able to be completely honest with myself right away. I went through a period of being too prideful to say that a piece of me really wanted my family to work. What I had to realize was that it was natural to feel that way. But it wasn't natural or healthy to raise a child in a situation that didn't allow me to be mentally or emotionally stable for her. So my honest moment was that I had to find the strength to heal from the hurt and heal from the break-up. I had to admit that if the family picture that I had painted in my head was so perfect, there would have never been a break – up to begin with; and that I would find the best days of my life on the other side of my broken heart, rejection, and disappointment. I had to paint a new family picture that reflected the reality of just me and my daughter and our extended family and friends.

So here are some honest truths for you:

1) **Being rejected hurts – but it doesn't determine your value.** One person's opinion of you doesn't define the value of your life. Even if you've been together for 20+ years and things have ended, every day that you wake up and are alive is a day that you have to add value to yourself.

2) **Broken Hearts Heal -** Don't stay within your S.A.D. emotions for too long. As you allow time to pass and start creating a life for yourself, you will heal from your deepest hurts and you will find yourself stronger and ready for the life that you were meant to live.

3) **Disappointment is part of the process not the destination –** It is okay to feel disappointed that things didn't work out as you had planned. It is **not** okay to live a life of disappointment. Life has a way of self-correcting- some of our greatest joy is a result of some of our greatest pain. We can gain a greater perspective and appreciation of our temporary trials. We may also gain the unique ability to help others who may find themselves in a similar situation.

If you are reading this, more than likely your honest truth is that you are now single, you have experienced an indescribable hurt, and you have a child(ren) that are depending on you. Process that information and give an honest account of how you feel. If you need to release some unresolved words or feelings toward your ex, do so in a healthy way. If you are in a situation that doesn't allow you to communicate with your ex or doesn't present a safe situation then write a letter and mail it, burn it, or rip it up but you have to release it to move on. It is that release that will free you to move forward with your new life. One important word of advice: the communication of your honest feelings is for YOU! It should only be done if you feel like there is something that you have to say to an ex that is keeping you from moving forward. Here is a warning: You can't communicate what you need to say with any expectations of how the other person will/ should respond. You can't be on a quest for them to validate or protect your emotions or feelings. You have to complete this step only when you are HONEST enough to say that their response has no direct relation to your self-esteem or self worth. It requires a level of emotional vulnerability and strength that you will find once you have processed and accepted the reality of your singleness.

While you are on the journey of emotional honesty, you have to be able to fully evaluate and identify your own weaknesses that may not be healthy for you and your interactions with others. You have to honestly seek out things you may need to change about yourself that might be hindering you from reaching your full potential. Not that you aren't awesome now but the quest for personal growth is one that we should seek daily. You have to keep it real with yourself about yourself. This is the only way that you will be able to sort out and compartmentalize your emotions in a healthy way. You can't obtain peace in your mind, body, and spirit if you can't honestly identify your emotions, strengths, and weaknesses.

Here are some steps to help you on the process of self-honesty.

Processing your unresolved feelings

1) In your journal, write down everything you may want to say to your ex if you didn't think you would be judged by your peers for it- your honest feelings about how you feel about them.

2) From that list above, identify anything that you think may keep you from moving forward with creating your new life and ask yourself if you or your ex died tomorrow, would you regret that you never told them anything from the list. (I suggest you keep it to just one or two items) but if you have more, then that is fine too.

3) Create a way that you can present the items without blaming or degrading the other person. You don't want this exercise to turn into another blame session. Focus on the "I" of it all. Use statements such as "I was hurt" and "I was angry" instead of "You made me mad" or "You hurt my feelings". Blaming puts people on the defense and quickly shuts down the conversation.

It may take some time to grow strong enough to complete this step. You have to complete some more of the self-strengthening steps before you are able to communicate with you ex. However, I would suggest getting the feelings out of your body and on paper as quickly as you can.

Identifying areas of personal improvement

I really don't have a magic formula for this. I think we all sort of know some things that we can work on even if we don't always like to fully embrace them. I'd start by asking some close friends what they think are some areas in which you could grow. Most of the times their responses will be some you have heard before or some that you have felt on the inside you need to work on. For the most part, their responses shouldn't come as a surprise or shock. Just remember that your change doesn't come over night, and personal growth is a process. You're on the the right path as long as you are making a daily effort to become a little better each day. Also remember that everyone has some personality weaknesses. The best thing that you can do is to be aware of them, but also work on sharpening your strengths.

5

APPRECIATION

The act of estimating the qualities of things and giving them their proper value: dictionary.com

I'd love to say that my whole life spiraled out of control all because ONE person lacked appreciation for me. However, the honest truth is that I lacked appreciation for those that loved and valued me; but most importantly, I lacked appreciation for MYSELF and all my gifts and talents. There was a lack of appreciation of me present in the relationship, and my thoughts stayed stuck on "How could he not appreciate all I'd done for him and our family?" I was blinded by my need to answer that question for way too long, and I wasn't able to fully see what was around me. I was missing the fact that there were many more people that loved, valued and appreciated me. There were people that were supporting, praying and believing that my daughter and I would succeed and I wasn't in the place to see or receive it.

I wasn't alone on the journey. There were people that were there for me through every step, challenge, defeat, and success that I had taken for granted. My circle of support was so much stronger than this one person, one challenge, and one setback and I had to draw strength from it. I had to dig deep down and recover the greatness that they all knew existed inside of me. I had to do so by remembering and appreciating even the smallest things that held such great value. Here are the top four things I had to learn to appreciate more so that I could rebuild a healthy life full of love, peace and joy.

1) **My child** – My daughter loved me unconditionally. It didn't matter to her the amount of money I had, the car I drove (or didn't for a long time), or where we lived. As long as were together, she was happy. I had to place her at the forefront of my mind; I had to learn to appreciate the gift of her, accept her unconditional love for me even when I messed up. I had to appreciate the honor I had to be her mother and what a great blessing it was to be able to have my legacy live through her and her children's children. The thought of that alone allowed me to realize that my destiny was larger than the temporary hurt and rejection that I was currently experiencing. I had an important job to do, one that would change generations and I needed to place all of my energy into impacting the world in a great way by being the best mother I could be. I needed to give my daughter her proper value in my life, and then live each day demonstrating to her exactly what that was. I had to become a source of unconditional love for her just as she was for me. When I committed to living everyday appreciating my daughter, I really didn't have time to think about anything else. The house began to feel warm again.

2) **My family** – My family was and is my biggest support and I often neglected that fact. My dad had allowed me and my daughter to live with him when things had gotten financially rough. He took on the task of showing my daughter how a man truly loves and cares for his family on a daily basis. I was blessed to be able to have a great example of a father, and now my daughter was doubly blessed to be able to experience his love and kindness. She is able to reap the benefits and love of a man that truly appreciates his family and allows her to be herself. It's a priceless gift that I can never repay fully, but I will spend the rest of my days trying. My mom has loved and supported me in the way that only mothers can: telling me the tough stuff, but loving me through the decisions I made whether I followed her advice or not, and comforting me through the tears and frustration and encouraging me to forgive myself for the times I got things wrong. She provided me the strength to be a mother at all times no matter what the situation. Most importantly she prayed for me. Her prayers protected me in ways I will never fully know. My sisters- well they were just themselves-making me laugh. They acted as childcare and transportation at times when I found myself lacking both. They were always there just loving me, supporting me and rooting for me to succeed. I often took their presence for granted thinking that's just what family does. The reality is that not everyone is so blessed to come from such a loving and supportive environment and I am thankful for the gift of my family. Without them, I don't know where I'd be and I had to begin to shift my focus to how awesome it was to have the unconditional love and support of my family. I had to put my energy into being a better daughter,

sister, and aunt so that I truly become the woman that I am destined to be. They are my constant core, and with them I can do anything I set my mind to accomplishing.

3) My Friends - I was always the go-to friend. The friend everyone turned to for advice. I was always able to provide an encouraging word or direct my friends to a helpful resource. So when I found myself as the one in need I really didn't know how to process or handle the returned support I got from my friends. I had become accustomed to helping everyone else; so it was hard for me to accept and appreciate the returned love and support that I was receiving from them. It was even harder to ask for help from them, but life has a way of breaking you down to build you for better. I felt that I had to act like everything was okay, like I had it all together. The truth is I didn't have to, not with my friends. When I found myself so broken that I couldn't even pretend anymore, they were shoulders to cry on, ears to listen, and cheerleaders to my many ventures, and childcare at times. They were all that I needed them to be and I am grateful for their support. Once I was able to truly appreciate their gift of friendship, love, and support, I was able to add that friend power to my family power as I began to re-build my life. I will spend my days striving to be the friend to them that they have been to me for all these years. New or old, a good friend is worth way more than gold.

4) **ME** – Once I was able to recognize and value the team of people that were supporting me, I began to believe that I had something great to offer others and people valued it. It was time that I started reclaiming my value and recognizing my worthy. I was priceless, irreplaceable, a one of a kind masterpiece. I was

created with unique strengths because I had something awesome to offer the world- a mission that only I could complete. As long as I kept looking at the closed door, I would never see the open door that held new opportunities, experiences, and new and exciting life.

Parenting while single has been one of my hardest yet fulfilling life challenges. It has broken me down to levels I never knew existed. It forced me to face weaknesses that I had successfully covered for years, but most importantly it allowed me the courage to boldly and honestly communicate exactly who I am to a very important person- ME. Once I really learned to love and appreciate who I am without apology, I was able to present myself to everyone I interacted with without apology and without shrinking. It was the appreciation of myself that set my spirit free to soar. The journey of parenting while single has taken me places I don't think I would have been bold enough to go without experiencing some of the darkness that the journey brings with it. I wouldn't have limitless faith and I wouldn't have taken bold risks, without the muscles I developed as a single parent.

The strength you develop once you have faced your biggest fear or your hardest challenges allows you to embrace and love yourself in a whole new way. I encourage you to take the time to make peace with who you are. Love and appreciate who you are and watch your world change for the better.

6

PRAYER

A devout petition to God or an object of worship: diction-ary.com

Prayer is the best thing that happened to me. Once I truly started praying for God's help, I was able to take on the challenges that life presented to me. I was able to change my response from anger to love. I was able to truly feel loved. I know that everyone has their own spiritual beliefs and it is not my intent to force mine upon you. However, I do know that in every spiritual/religious practice, prayer and meditation is at the center. It was through prayer that I was able to unload the weights that were holding me down. It was through prayer that I was able to express things that I couldn't verbalize to another human being and it was through prayer that I was able to find a peaceful escape from the challenges of life.

As you can see, prayer wasn't my first go-to option. I tried a lot of unproductive paths before I truly committed myself to praying. It honestly wasn't until things really seemed bleak that I truly committed to making prayer a consistent part of my lifestyle. I encourage you not to wait as long as I did but I also assure you that it is never too late to start. I was able to connect with my God in a greater way, and He was able to heal my wounds and strengthen my soul. I began to view my situation as more of a learning process and less of a punishment.

One thing that I learned was that I had to be honest about my feelings in prayer and ask God to remove the negative thoughts and mindsets that had crippled me for so long. I had to begin to pray before I acted, pray before I spoke, and pray before I interacted with my ex. It was when I adopted the attitude that I could do nothing without praying, that I started to see change.

I have to be honest; I started off praying for God to change my ex. That was my daily thing for a good long while. Lord, make him do this, that and everything else. I soon had to change my prayers because I only began to frustrate myself when I saw no change. So I began to pray for a change in me-to make me a better person, a better mother, a better family member, a better friend, and a better co-parent. I left changing the hearts of others in the hands of God. I asked Him to show me His way and what I needed to do in order to live the life that He created me to live. It is my spiritual belief that we are all created with a purpose and that everything we experience even through the results of our disobedience and rebellion is a way to bring us closer to God. He knows exactly what we are going to do before we decide to do it and it's His plan to work it out for our good. We have to recognize it and accept it no matter how hard we think it gets. One thing I have learned is that God is with us through all things but He will never force Himself upon us.

When we are ready to acknowledge Him, He will be there to guide us. As I opened my mouth and heart to pray, I began to see a change- a change that gave me the strength to push forward, to face my fears, pursue my dreams and to rebuild and love my life and all those within it.

I encourage you to make prayer or meditation a part of your lifestyle. It is the only way that you will truly see change, peace and love fill your life.

Tips on how to get started in prayer

1) **Prayers don't have to be long and drawn out** – Most people think that praying is this great production. It's not. All you have to do is start a conversation. Be honest with your feelings and ask for help removing all things that aren't beneficial to and for you. Admit that you need help and seek forgiveness for any missteps. In my S.A.D. days my prayers were as simple as "please help me."

2) **Pray daily** – I encourage you to pray daily and often multiple times per day. I found that waking up about 15 minutes early to start my day in prayer was helpful. I prayed at lunch and before bed. The more I prayed, the more I wanted to pray and it became part of my daily life.

3) **It's not always instant but it's always working** – When I truly committed to prayer, I didn't always see the answer to my prayers in the timeframe that I thought I should and it became a little frustrating. However, once I removed the time limits, I began to see the effects of

consistent time spent in prayer. So I adopted the motto that even though you may not see instant results, your prayers are always working and their results will manifest exactly when you need them.

So challenge yourself! Why not test out the idea to see if it works for you? My challenge is to try it. Embark on a 30 day prayer trail. Commit to praying in the morning and night for 30 days and see if you feel, act and perceive life differently.

7

PURPOSE

The reason for which something exists or is done, made, used, etc.: dictionary.com

Once I began to incorporate prayer in my life, I had the strong desire to really want to know what my purpose was in life. I didn't just want to sit around and wait for life to happen; I wanted to be begin doing whatever it was that I was born to do. I had a strong sense that I would find joy in my life once I discovered my purpose. Once I started actively living it, I would find the life, happiness, joy and love that God has for me.

Everyone has a different journey, and a unique life to discover and I encourage you to ask for direction and clarity for yours during your 30 day prayer challenge. You will come to a realization and understanding of what your purpose is, and then small downloads of assignments to complete your destiny. The assignments will come as you begin to complete them. The thing about purpose is that you have to be actively living it and most of the time it is connected to your challenges. As you complete the assignments, you will begin to attract the people, resources and strength you need to accomplish your task. I do have to warn you that following your purpose isn't always easy. You might be faced with making some choices that make you look crazy to the outside world but do it anyway. If you know this is what you are created to do, don't stop until it is done. I've had to make some pretty radical choices that didn't always lead to the most lucrative lifestyle but they always got me one step closer to my purpose. Most importantly, my needs and my daughter's needs have always been met.

My one word of advice is to guard your purpose. It's not to be shared with everyone because everyone won't understand or support it. There will be plenty of people who will have their opinions of what they think you should do. I challenge you to stay focused, determined, appreciative, humble and hardworking.

Once you discover exactly what you were meant to do with your time here on earth, your decisions will become easier to make. Life challenges will be lighter to bear because you know that your one focus is to fulfill your purpose and everything else is just fuel to help you complete it. I encourage you to create a vision board of what you want your life to look like and things you'd like to accomplish. Place it in a highly visible location in your home so that you can consistently be reminded of what you are working toward. I first came across the concept of vision boards while watching the movie The Secret. The vision board is such a powerful tool. I find myself looking back on some of my early vision boards and I am amazed at how many images I've posted that have now become my realities.

8

YOU

The nature or character of the person addressed: diction-ary.com

During this journey of single parenting, we often lose sight of who we are. We spend our days so focused on meeting the needs of our children and keeping up with our work commit-ments that we lose sight of how great we are as individuals. I had lost myself in my situation and as I moved through my journey for happiness, I began to rediscover who I was. I had to remind myself that I had value, that I had talents and that I had potential to do anything I set my mind to do.

The more I prayed, the more I discovered that God loves me, flaws and all. I actually began to recognize that since He created me, He already knew exactly what those flaws were. I decided to focus on my strengths because we become that in which we focus. The more we focus on our weaknesses, the weaker we become.

It's great to be able to identify your weaknesses and know what they are, but they don't define you. You have to accept all the quirky things that make you, you. The truth is that your friends and family love and accept you for who you are and now it's time for you to fully accept you for YOU. It's always good to focus on how you can grow, but the best thing you can ever do for yourself is love yourself at every moment.

Accepting who you truly are will allow you to really define your values and set boundaries. As a result, you will make smarter, wiser decisions that put you in position to improve your life. Accepting yourself allows you to fully be a better parent. You can better love and accept your child(ren) for all their unique qualities. If you're looking to date again, acceptance gives you the opportunity to better know what type of person may best interest you. It opens up your mind to loving someone flaws and all just like you want to be loved. You will also avoid wasting your time with people who you're not compatible with. You will be able to boldly and confidently express your needs within your new relationship allowing for a stronger foundation.

My last challenge to you is to look in the mirror everyday for the next 21 days and say "I love you!" three times per day. You may notice that the length of this challenge is slightly different from the 30 day prayer challenge. I believe it takes 21 days to create a habit and 30 days to create a lifestyle. I want you to get in the habit of loving yourself while creating a lifestyle of prayer and meditation. As you begin to express that you love yourself daily, you will begin to believe it and more importantly you will begin to act like it. You will be able to embrace YOU and embark on living a more joy-filled, love-filled, purpose-filled life for you and your children.

BE H.A.P.P.Y.

ABOUT INGRID M. WILLIAMS

Ingrid began her career in Human Resources and has over 8 years of experience working for several Fortune 500 companies. Ingrid left the Human Resources field to establish an event planning company and it was through that venture that she found her passion. As she planned community events with a local non-profit agency, she found that her calling was to help build strong communities, by assisting some of the weakest of its members gain strength. Through her community work, Ingrid has built an extensive network that allows her to connect individuals with the resources that they need to build an abundant life. Ingrid holds Bachelor's degrees in both Sociology and Labor Studies from Rutgers, The State University of New Jersey–Douglass College. Ingrid is the proud mother of a spunky, creative, smart, and beautiful daughter.